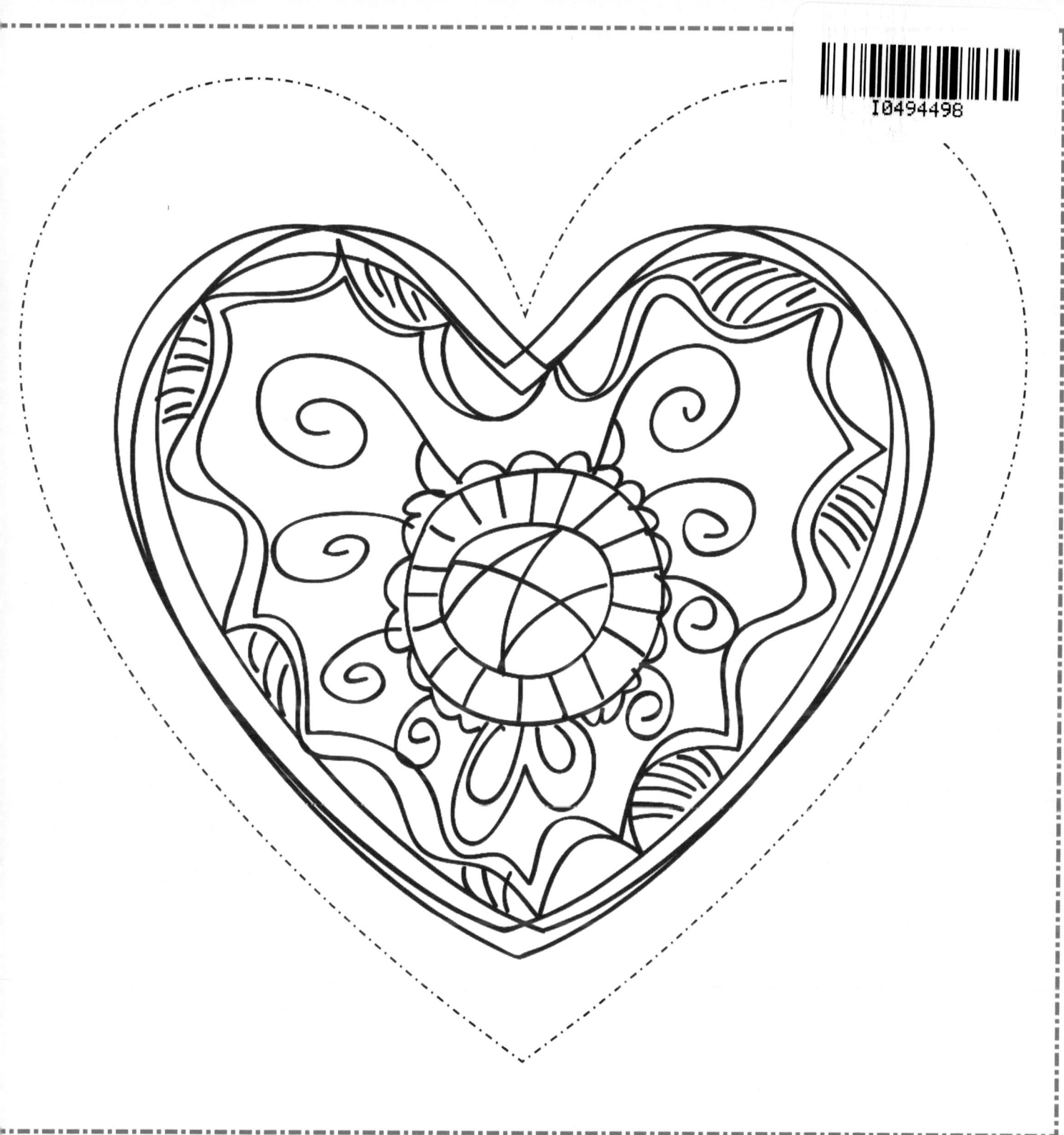

Be My Valentine!

To:

From:

Be My Valentine!

To:

From:

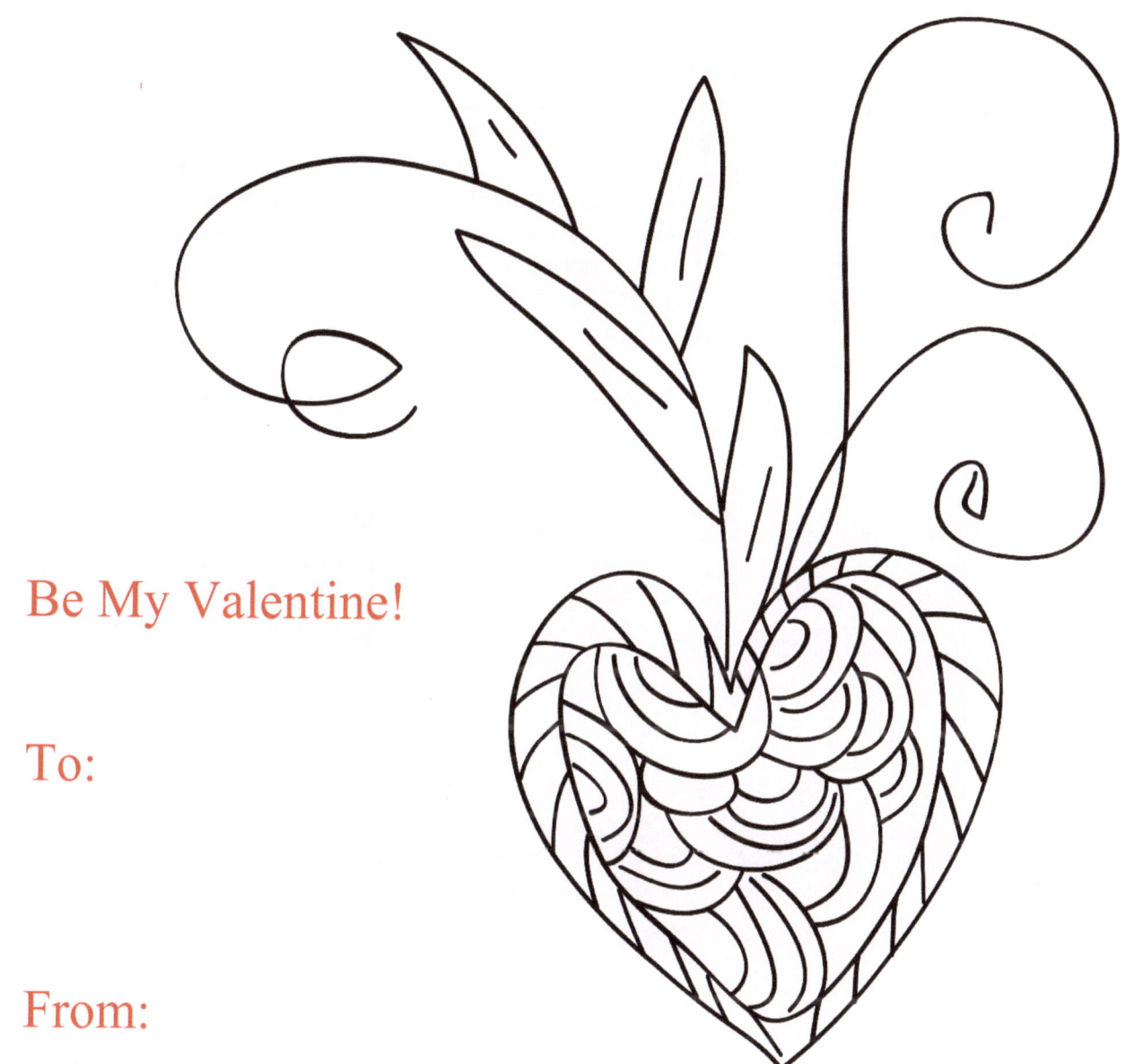

Be My Valentine!

To:

From:

I
LOVE
YOU

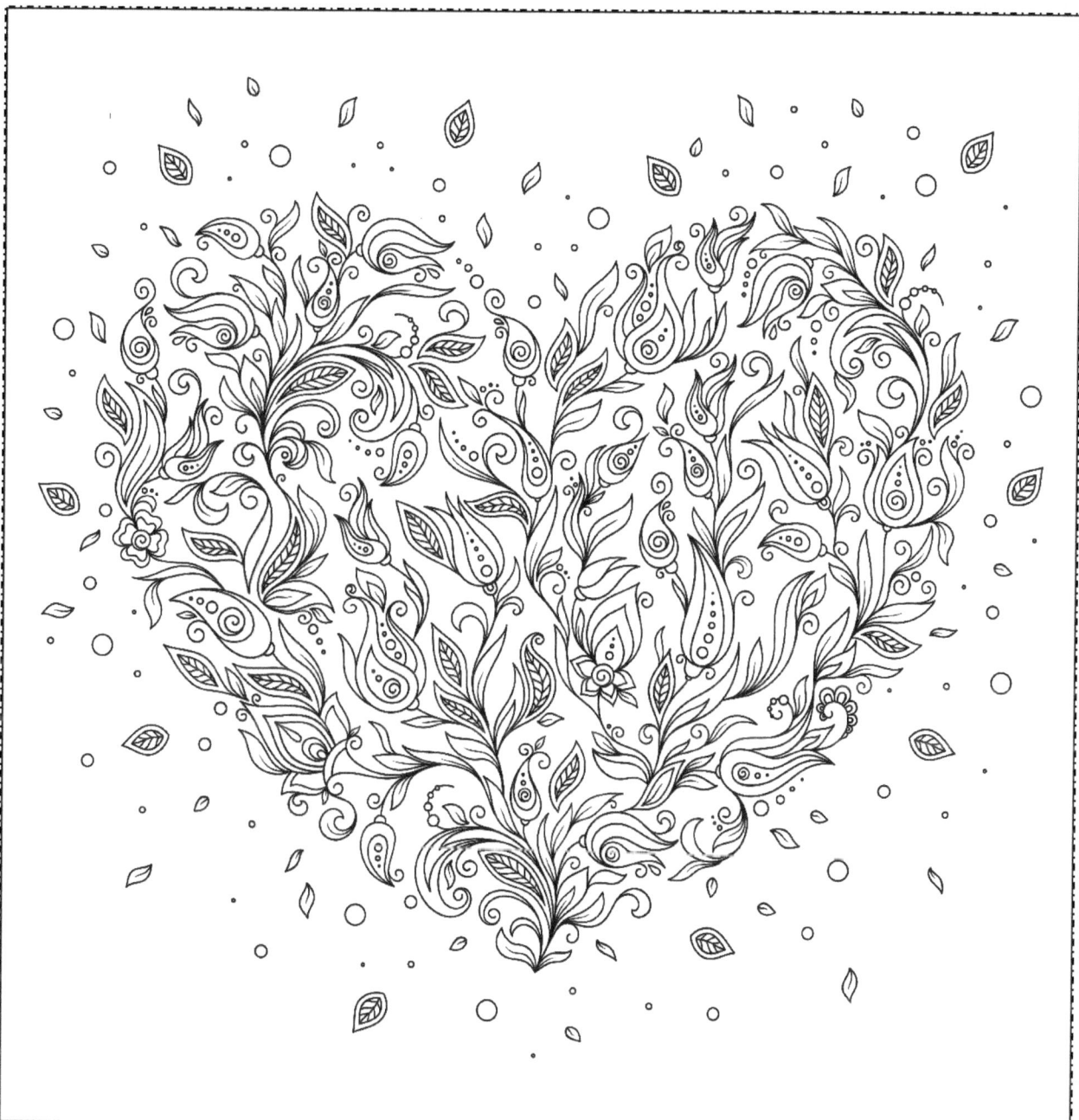

Be My Valentine!

To:

From:

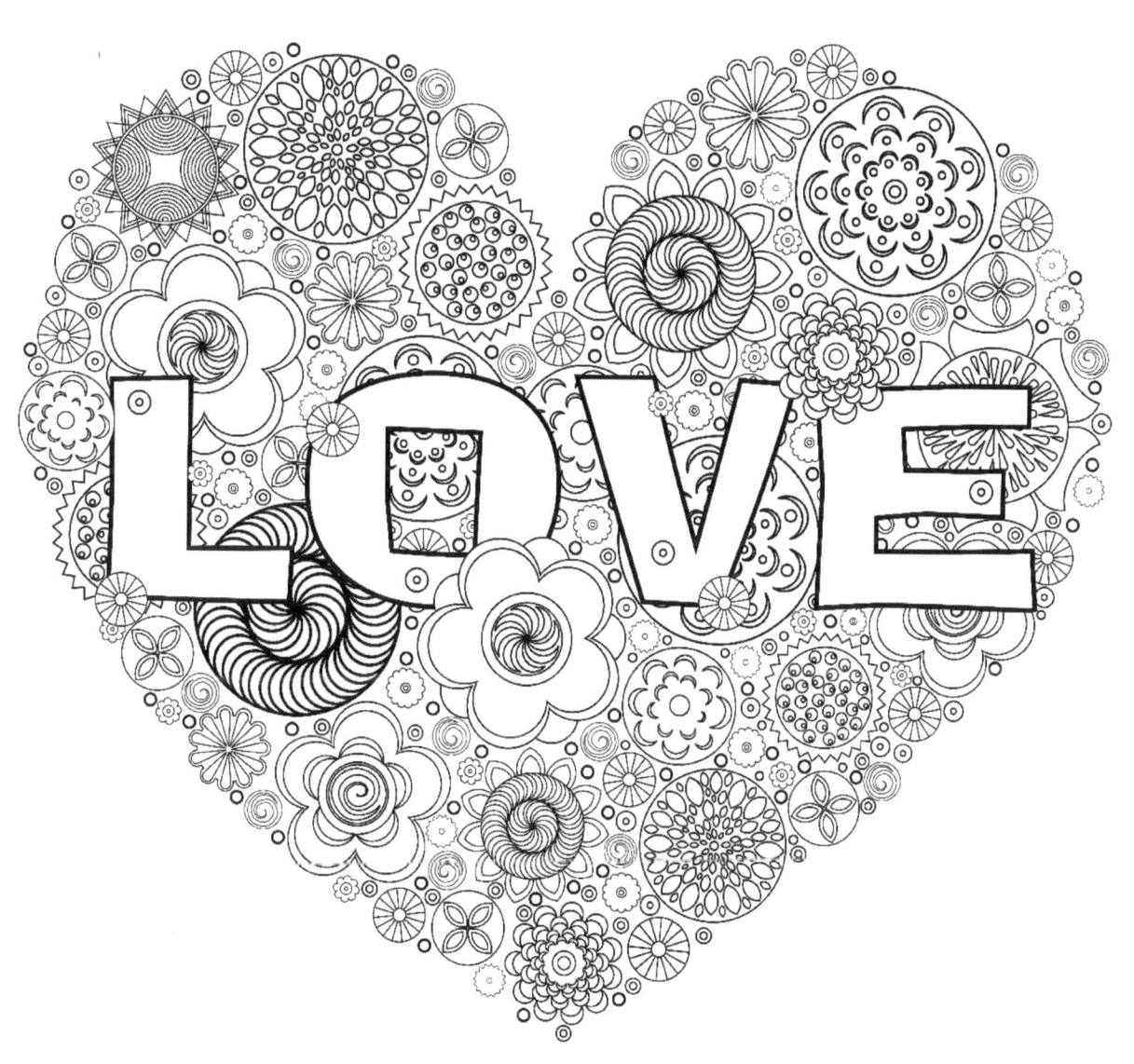

Be My Valentine!

To:

From:

Be My Valentine!

To:

From:

Be My Valentine!

To:

From:

Be My Valentine!

To:

From:

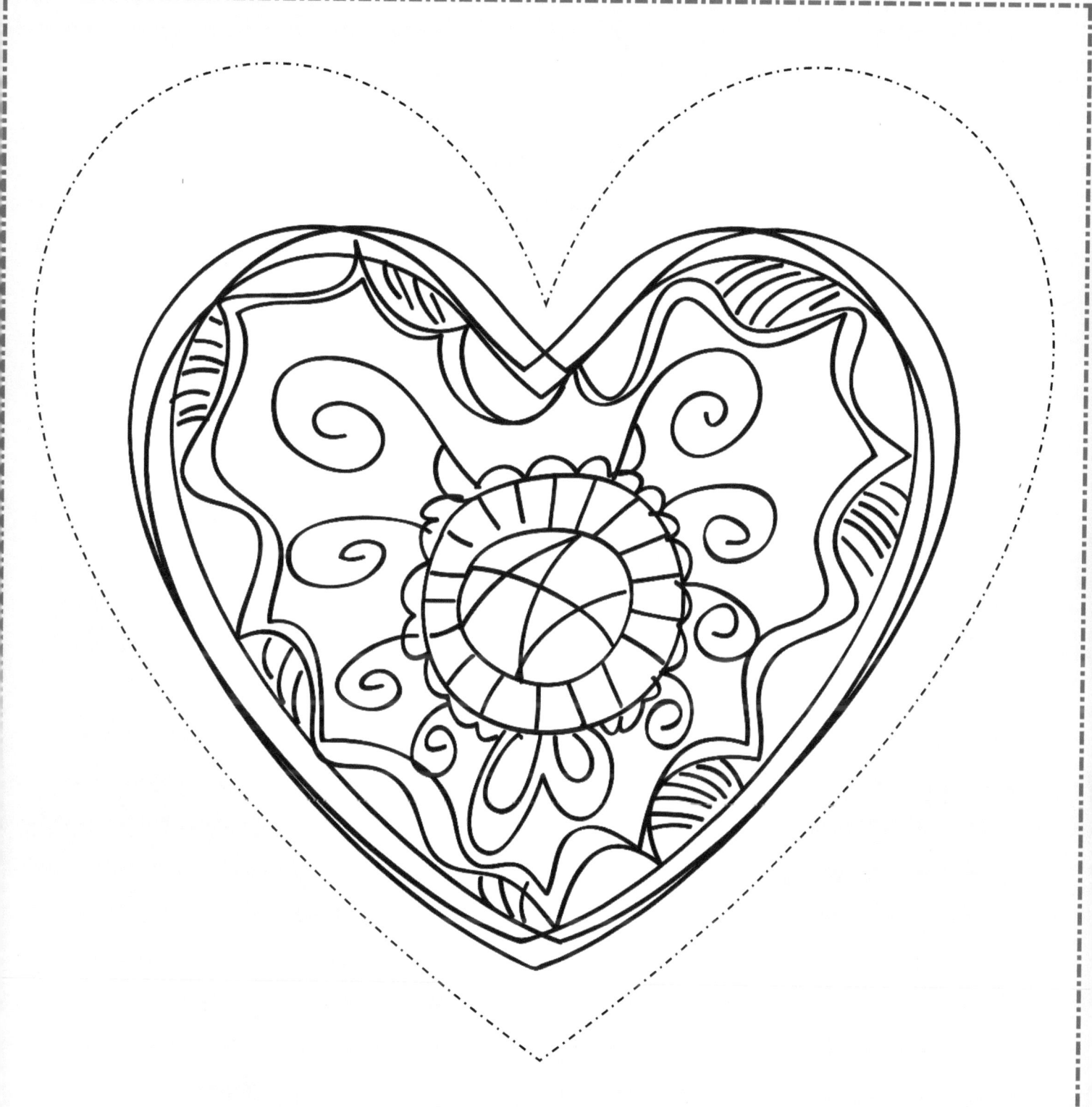

Be My Valentine!

To:

From:

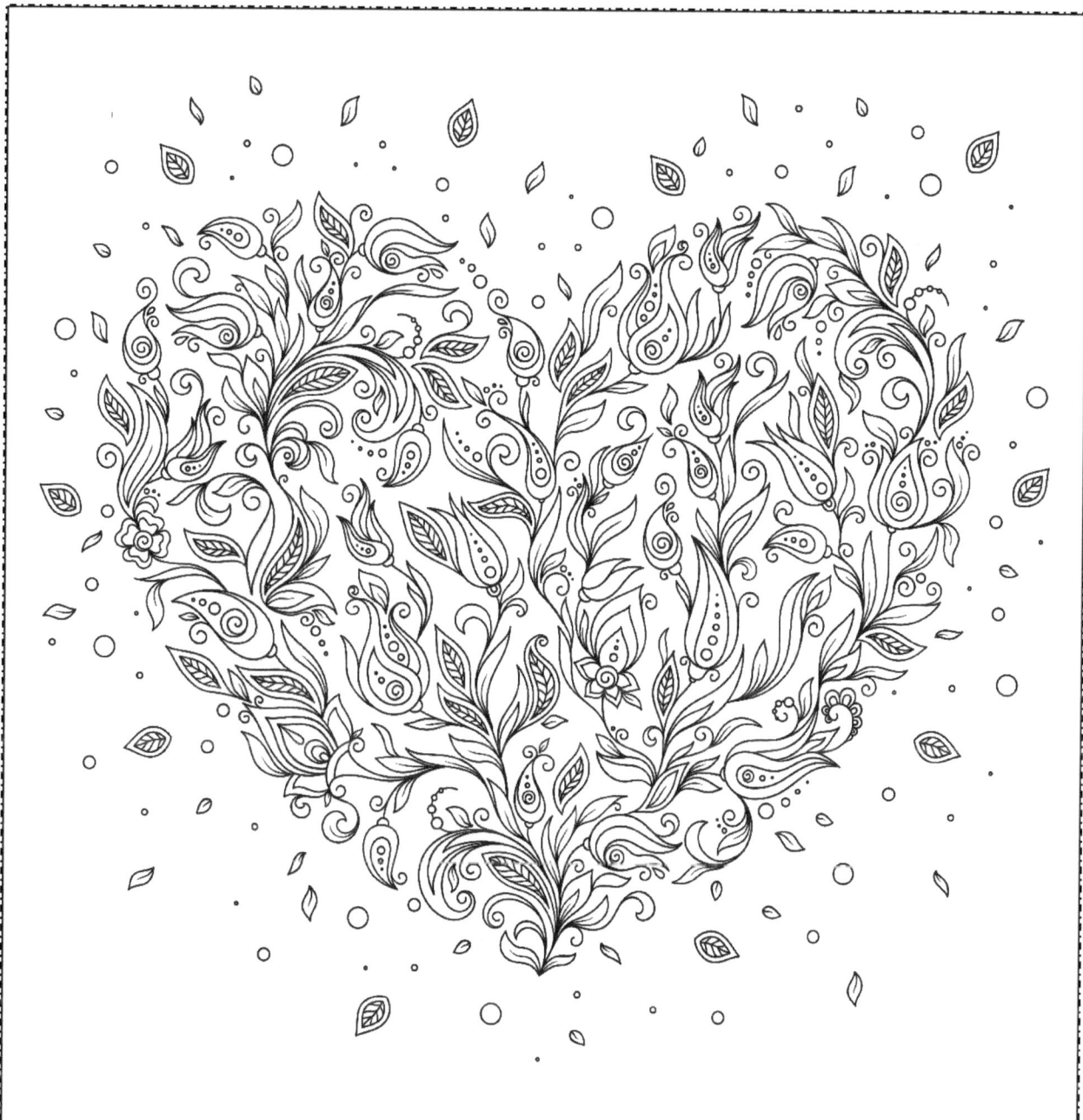

Be My Valentine!

To:

From:

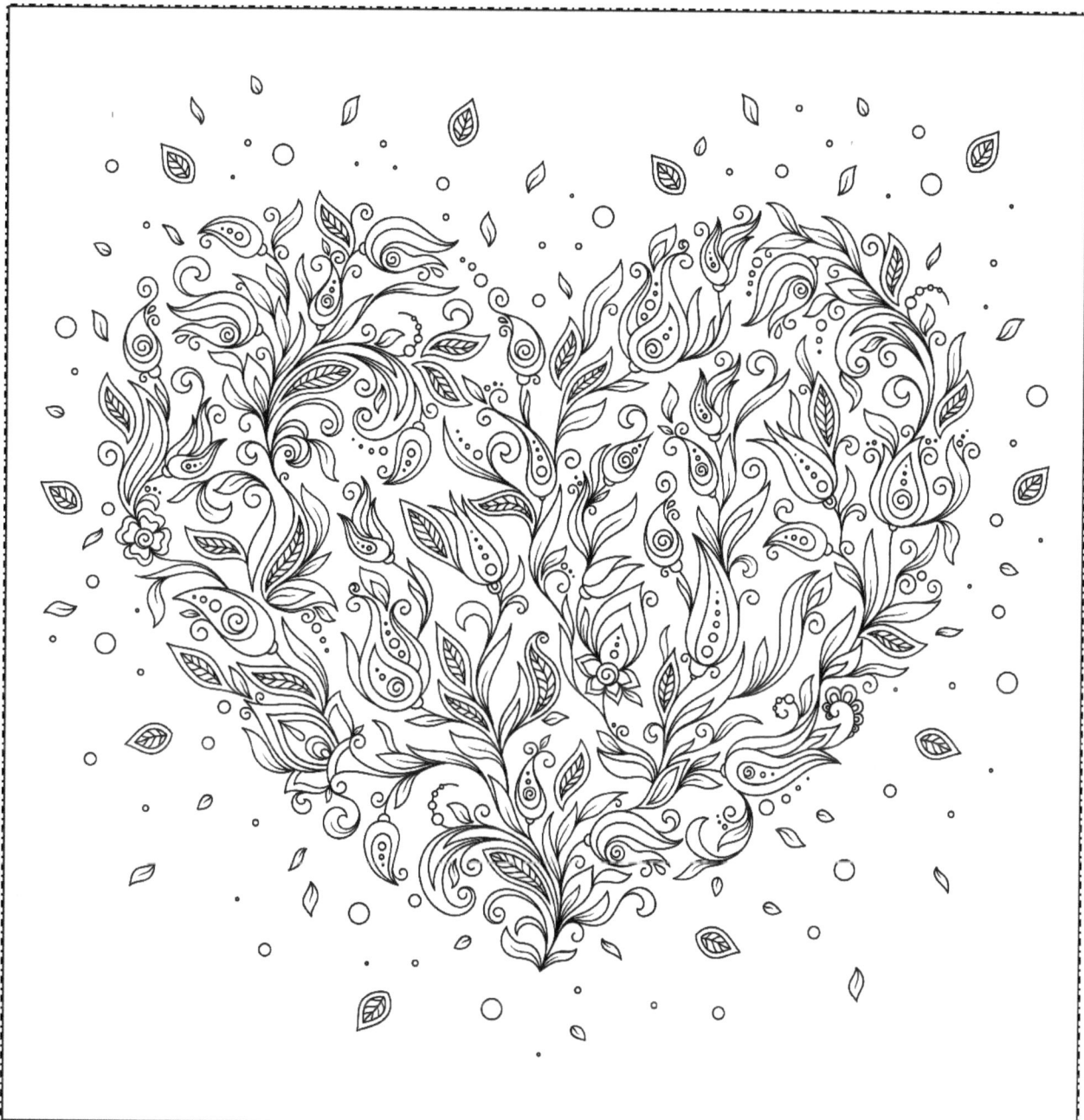

Be My Valentine!

To:

From:

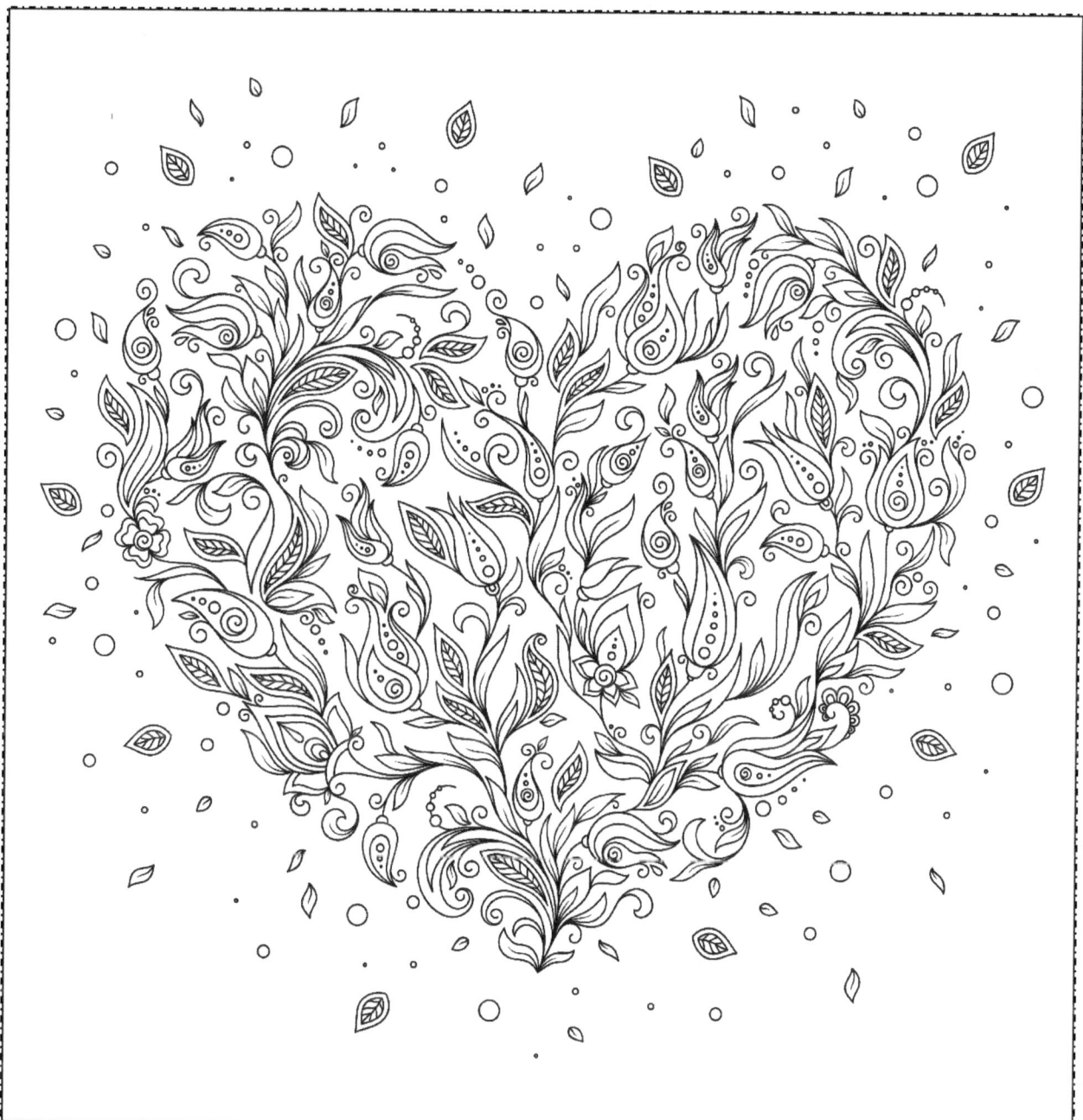

Be My Valentine!

To:

From:

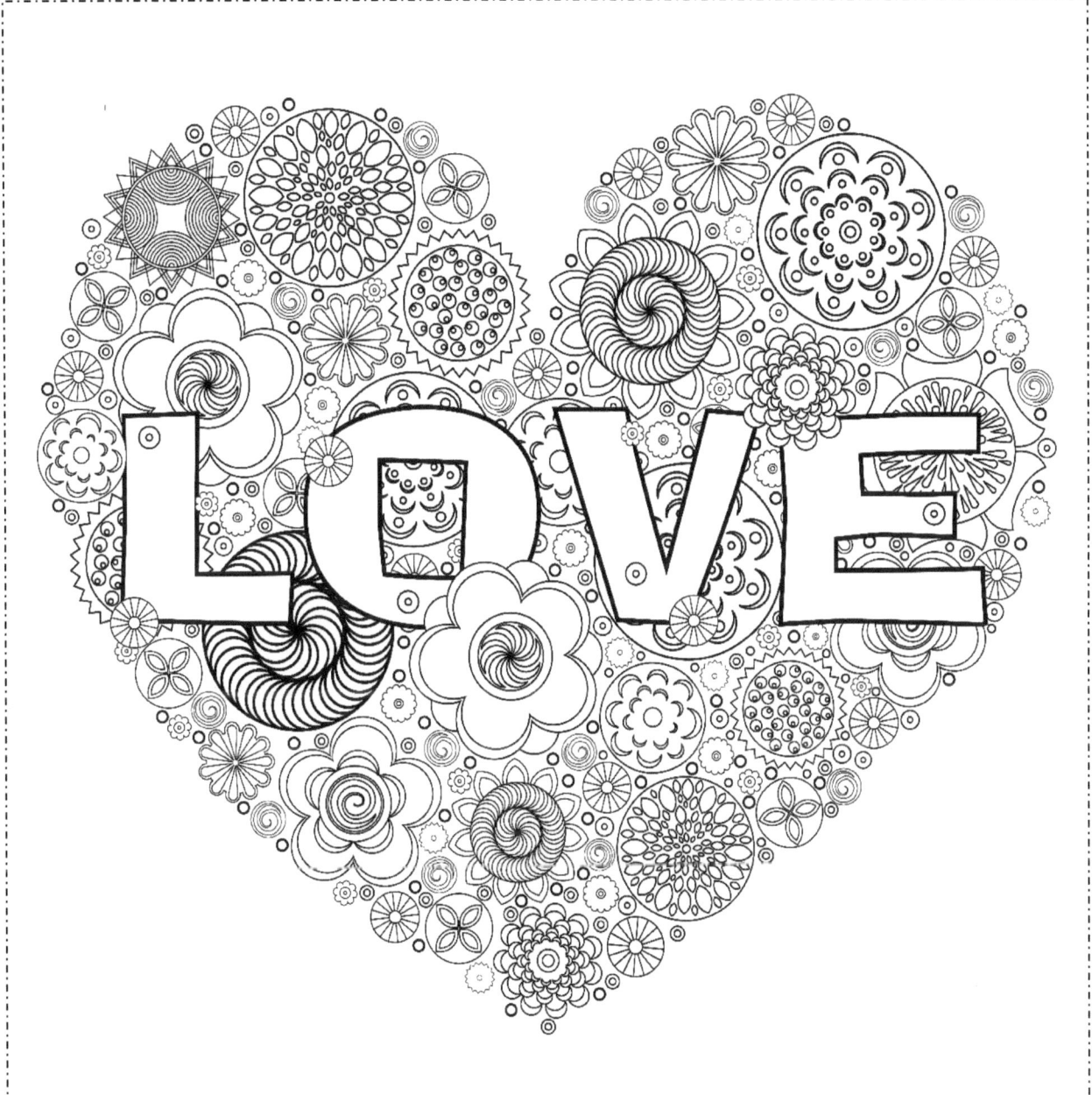

Be My Valentine!

To:

From:

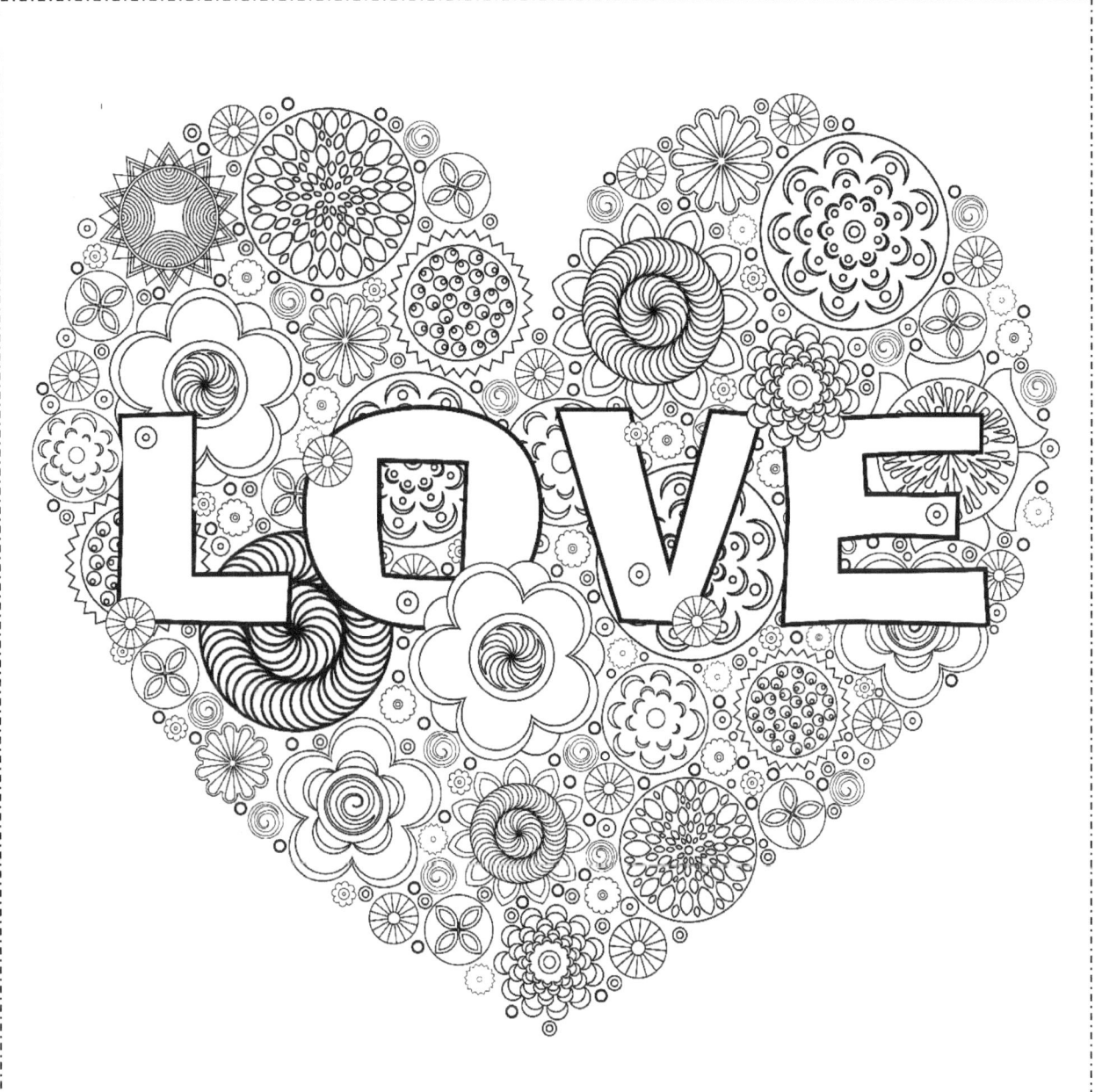

Be My Valentine!

To:

From:

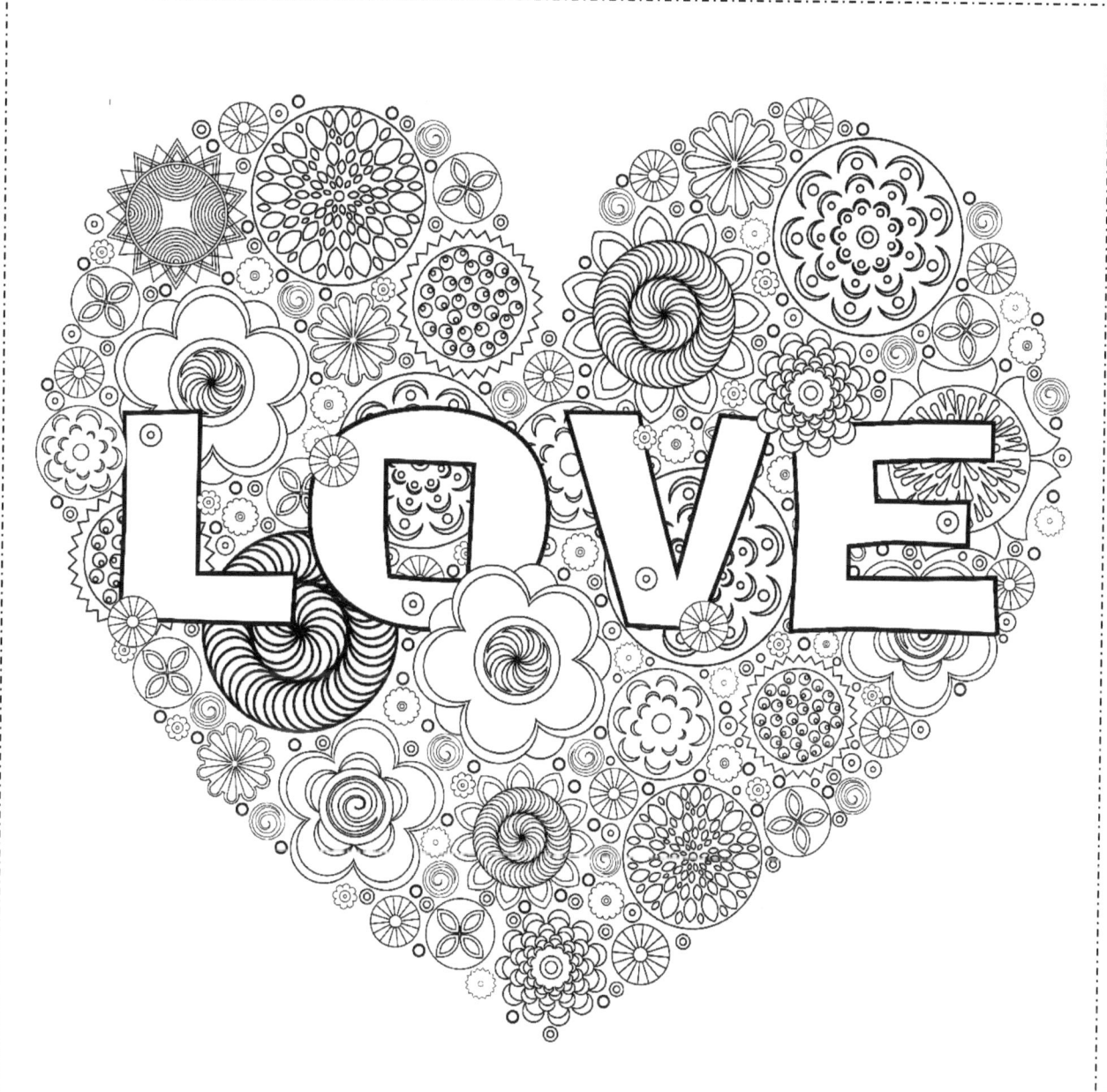

Be My Valentine!

To:

From:

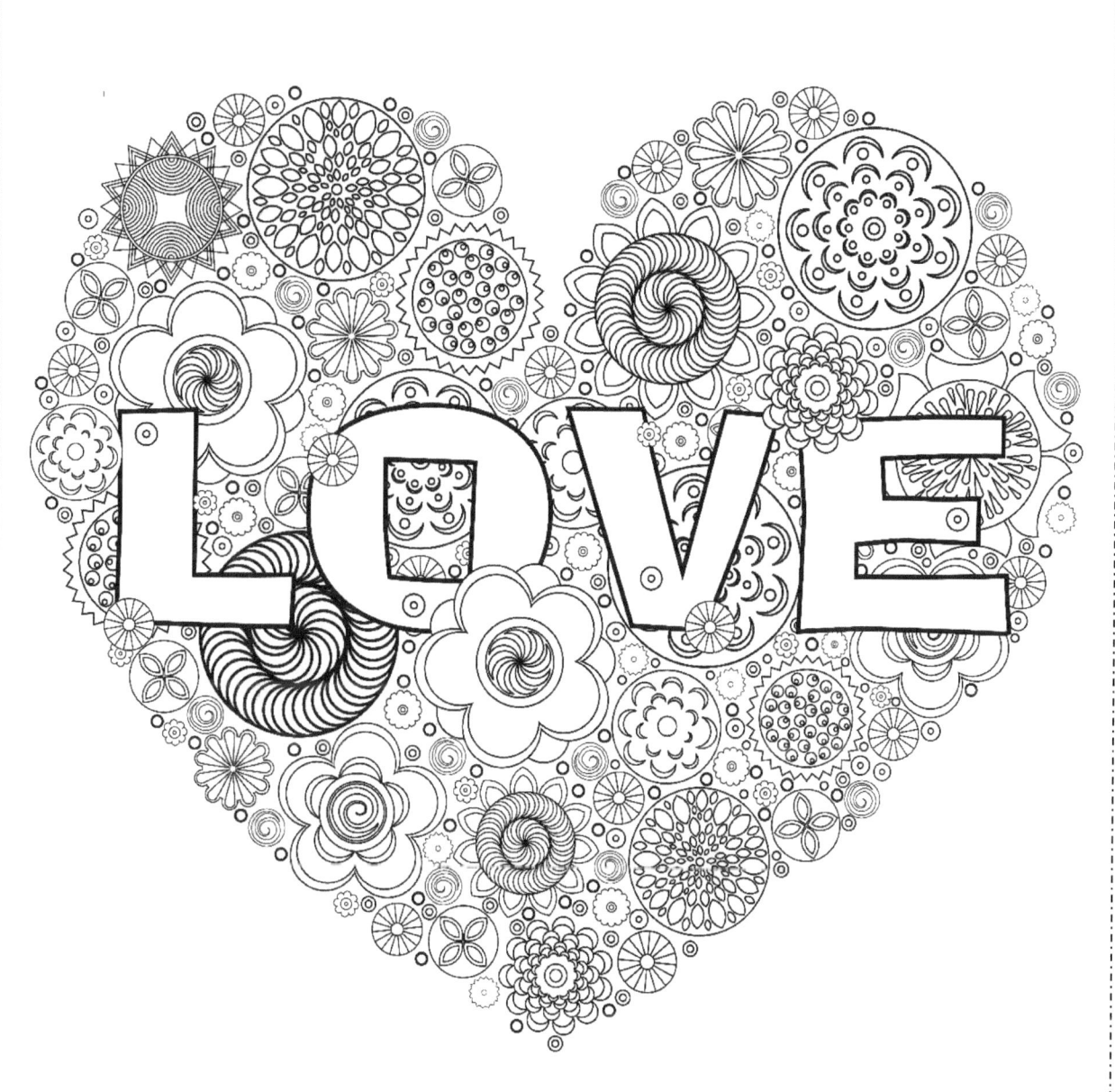

Be My Valentine!

To:

From:

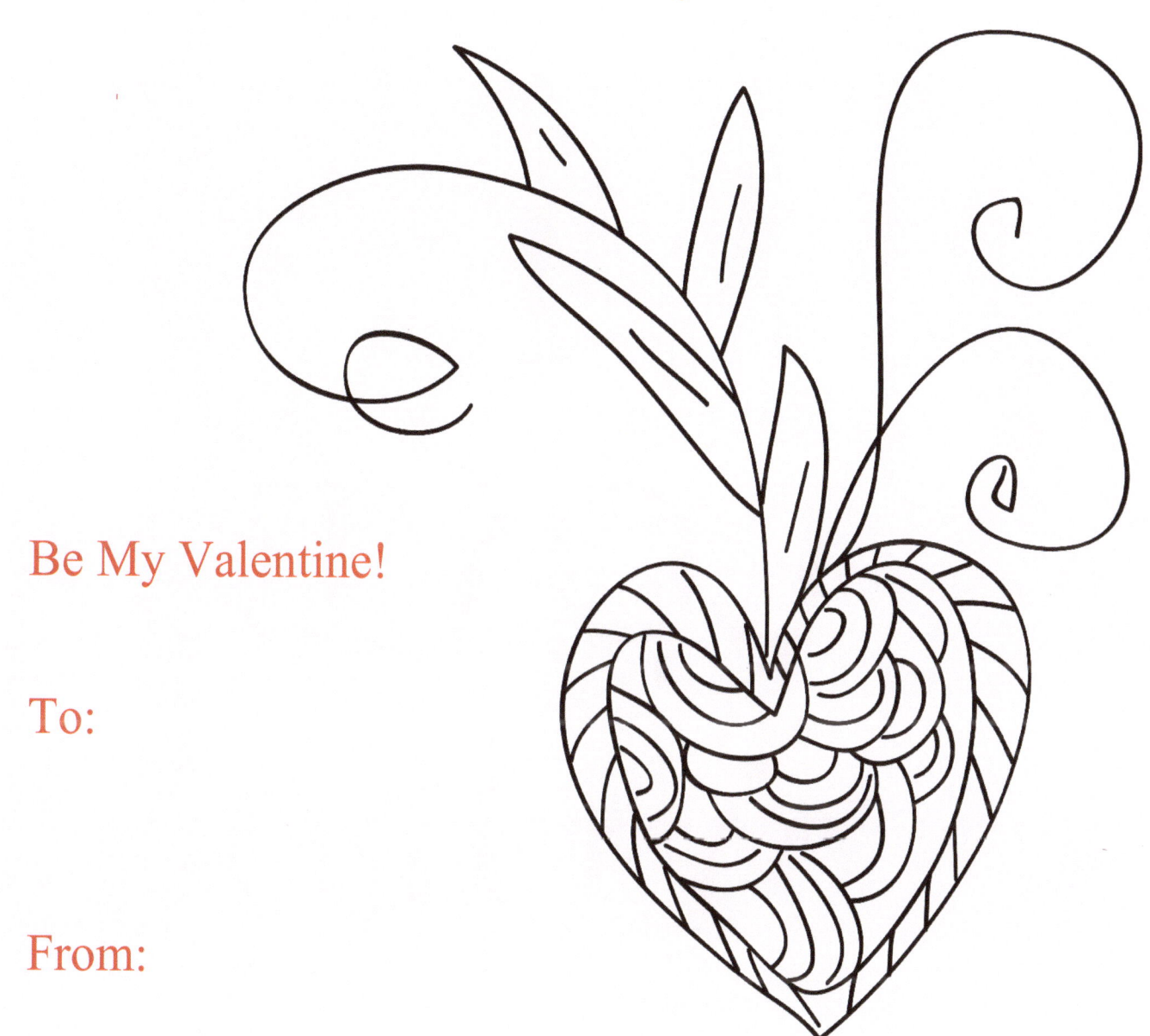

Be My Valentine!

To:

From:

I

LOVE

YOU

Be My Valentine!

To:

From:

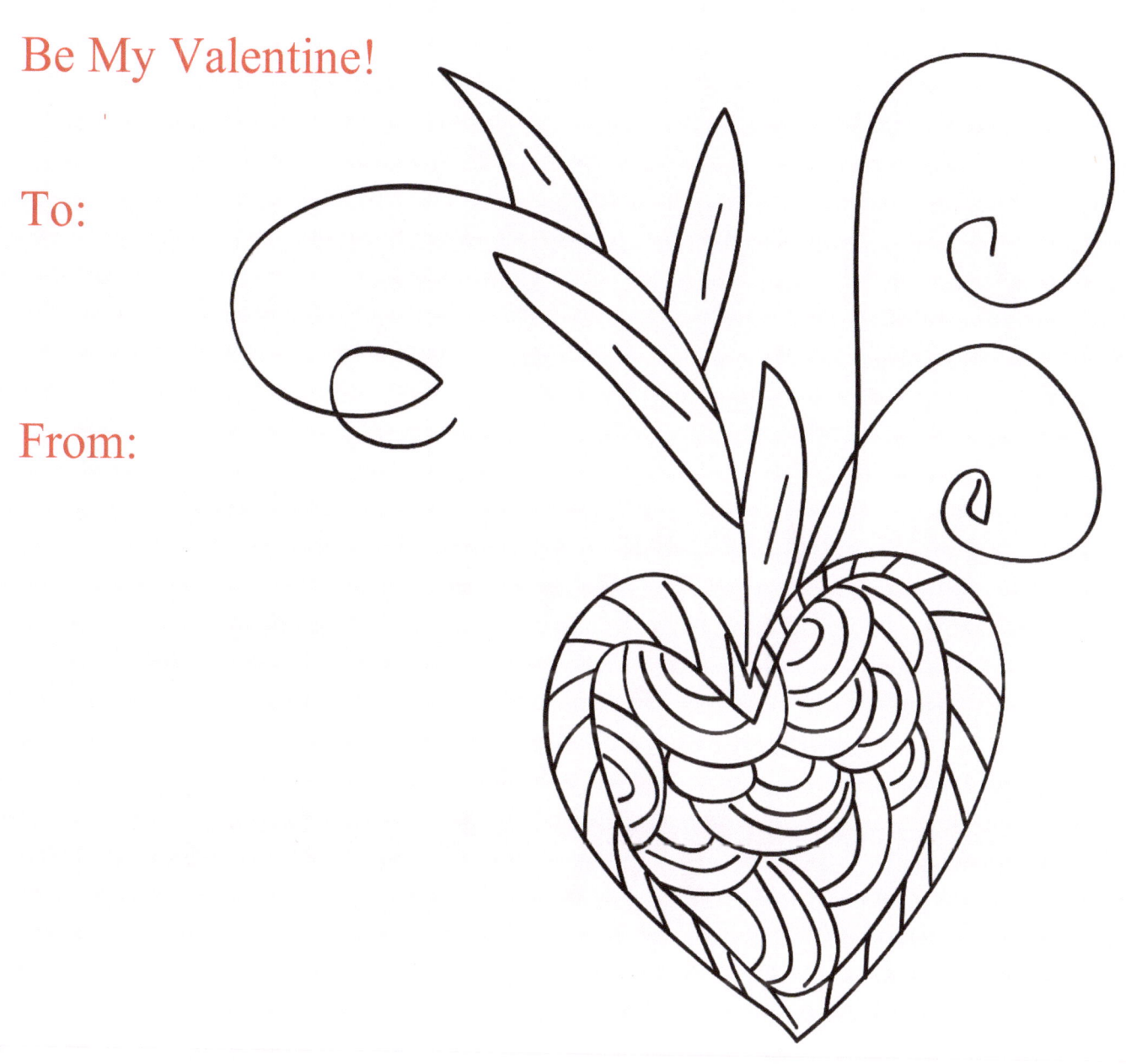

I

LOVE

YOU

Be My Valentine!

To:

From:

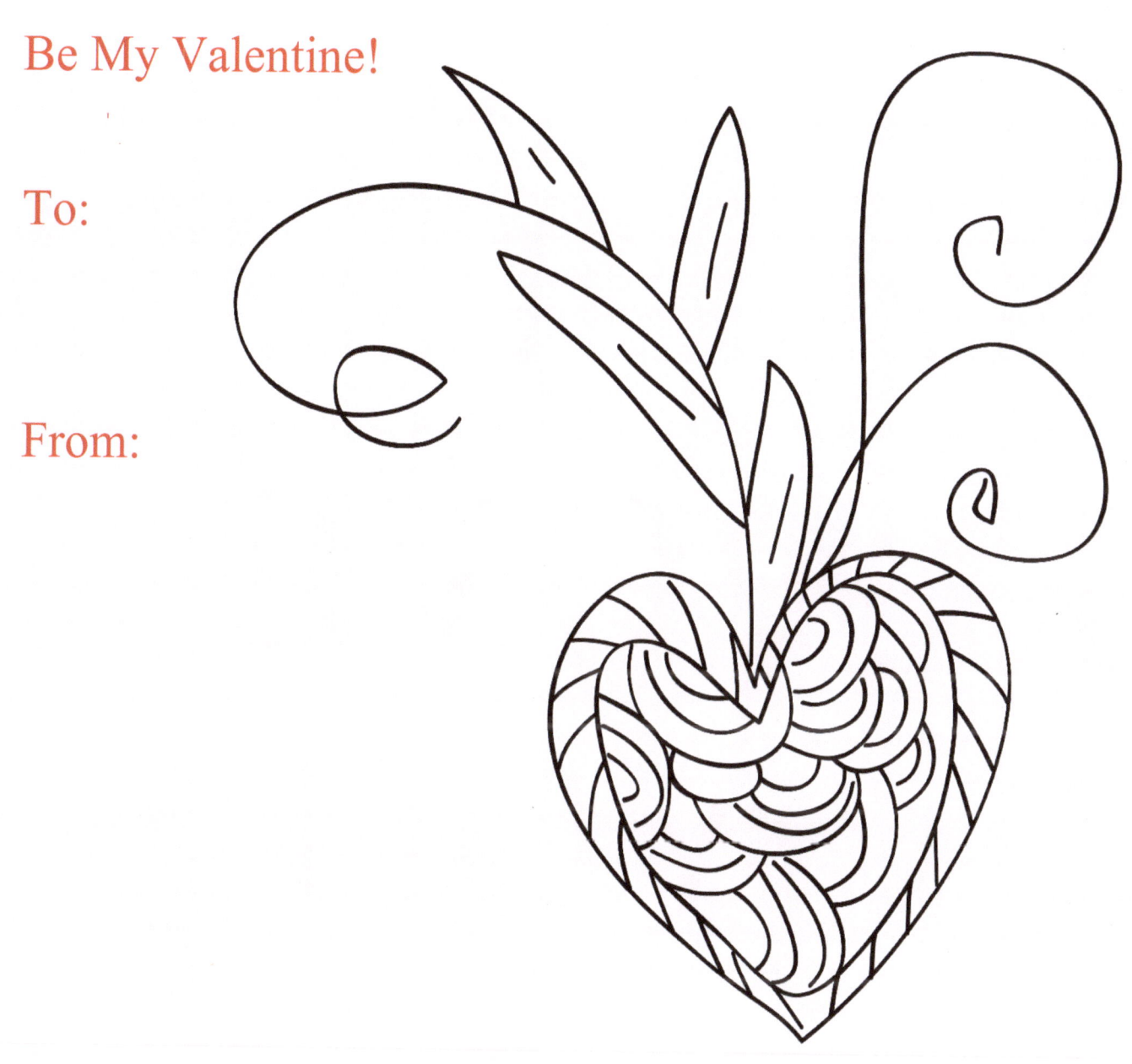

I
LOVE
YOU

Be My Valentine!

To:

From:

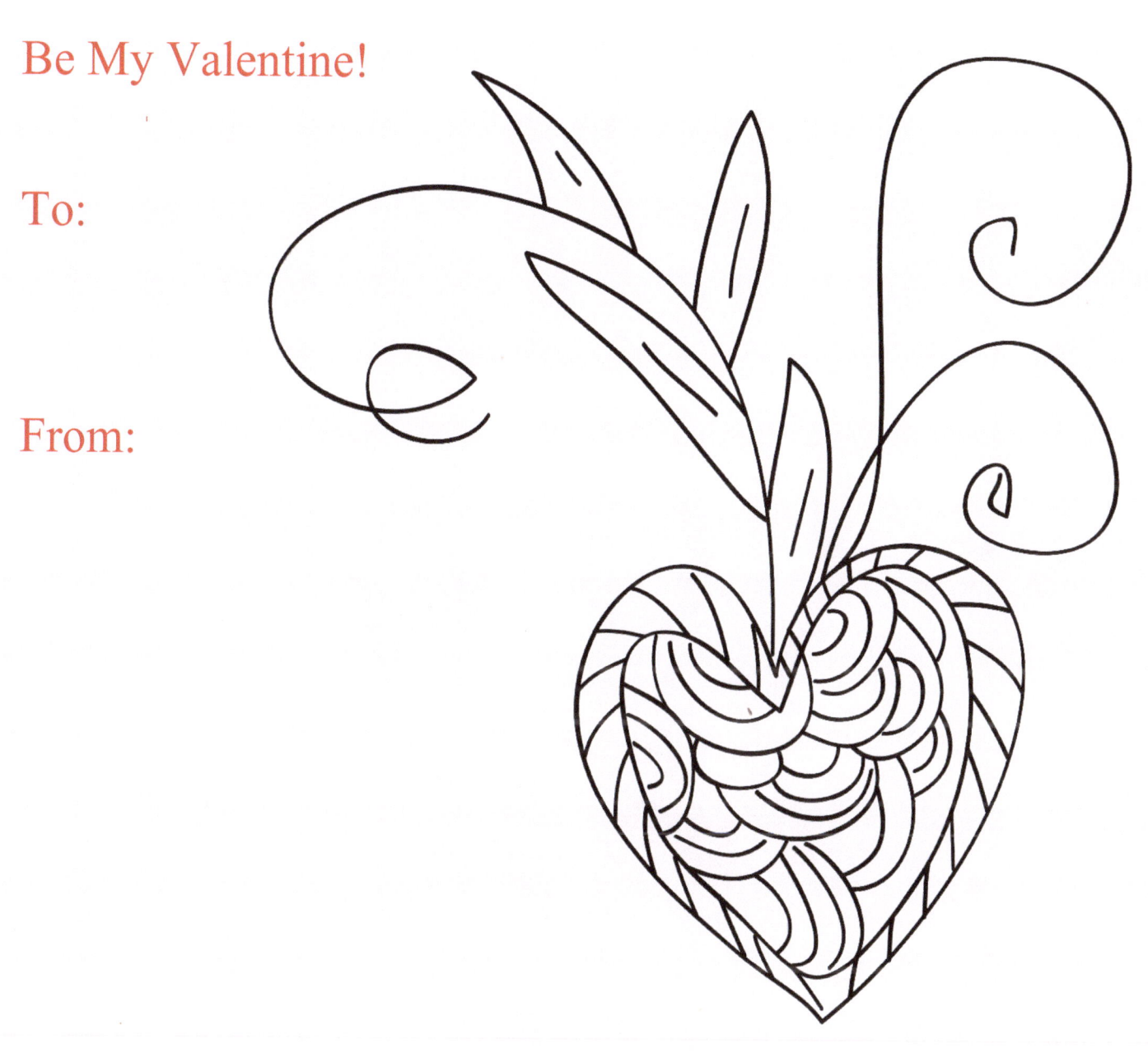

I
LOVE
YOU

www.ingramcontent.com/pod-product-compliance
Lightning Source LLC
Chambersburg PA
CBHW050841180526
45159CB00004B/1979